# What's it like to me?

# Religious Buildings

Anita Ganeri

HODDER
*Wayland*

an imprint of Hodder Children's Books

# Contents

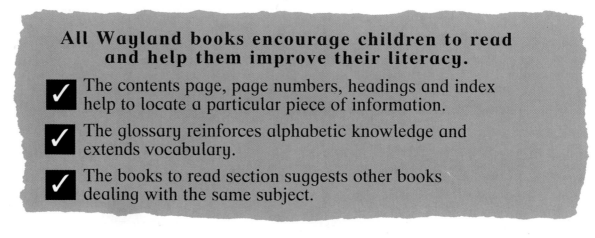

**All Wayland books encourage children to read and help them improve their literacy.**

✓ The contents page, page numbers, headings and index help to locate a particular piece of information.

✓ The glossary reinforces alphabetic knowledge and extends vocabulary.

✓ The books to read section suggests other books dealing with the same subject.

# Special Buildings

Do you have a favourite building or place? It might be your home or a place you go to on holiday. Why is it so special to you?

There are many special religious buildings. They are places where people go to worship and to learn more about their **beliefs**.

# Temples and Towers

These children are standing outside a Hindu mandir. This is a building where Hindus go to **worship**, meet their friends and learn about their **faith**. A mandir is also called a temple.

Mandirs do not have to be large buildings. This is a mandir on a busy street. People stop to worship on their way to school or work. Hindus believe that a mandir is a home for God on Earth.

Some mandirs have tall entrance towers, similar to this one. These towers are called gopurams. They are decorated with brightly coloured images of gods and goddesses. These are believed to protect the mandir from harm.

The city of Varanasi on the River Ganges in India is very special for Hindus. They bathe in the **holy** river because they believe its water will wash away their **sins**. There are lots of mandirs along the river bank.

# Meeting for Worship

A synagogue is a building where Jewish people meet to worship and learn about their faith. Some synagogues are very old. Others, like this one, are modern.

Inside the synagogue there is a raised
platform called a bimah. This is where
the holy **scrolls** are placed for reading.
The **congregation** all sit round it. In
many synagogues, men and women
sit apart.

Jewish weddings often take place in the synagogue. The bride and groom stand under a **canopy**, called a huppah. It is like a roof. It stands for the home they will share when they are married.

This is the Western Wall in Jerusalem.
Jewish people come here from all over the
world to pray. The wall is all that was left of
the Jews' ancient Temple when it was
destroyed two thousand years ago. The
Temple was the Jews' most holy place.

# Shrines and Stupas

Buddhists worship in a building called a vihara. This is also a place where Buddhist **monks** and **nuns** live. Many viharas have a meeting hall, rooms for teaching and **meditation** and a library.

When Buddhists visit the vihara, they take
off their shoes and go into the shrine room
to pay their **respects** to the Buddha. They
put their hands together and kneel in front
of the Buddha.

 This building is called a **stupa**. The first stupas were built to remember the Buddha. Others are for remembering important Buddhists. The eyes on the tower are the Buddha's eyes, keeping watch over the whole world.

Some Buddhist viharas in Japan have a sand garden, like this one. It is a very quiet, peaceful place. Looking at the garden helps the monks to think calmly and clearly about things that really matter to them.

# Going to Church

For Christians, a church is a very special building. This is where they meet to worship. Churches can be large or small, old or new. A cathedral, like this one, is a large, important type of church.

Inside this church, people sit on long benches called pews. The **altar** is at the far end. On the left is the pulpit, where the priest or minister gives a talk. The church is decorated with crosses, candles, paintings and beautiful stained glass windows.

Some people live in religious buildings. Christian monks live in a monastery. Nuns live in a convent. These buildings are peaceful places where monks and nuns can worship, work and praise God.

This grand church is called St Peter's **Basilica** in the Vatican City in Rome. The Vatican is very important as a place of pilgrimage for Roman Catholics. The Pope, the head of the Roman Catholic Church, lives in the Vatican.

# Mosques and Minarets

This is a mosque, a building which Muslims use specially for worship. The mosque has a dome and a tall tower called a minaret. From here, Muslims are called to say their prayers.

No statues or pictures are allowed inside a mosque. Instead, mosques are decorated with beautiful patterns and writing.

This verse reads:
'Neither slumber overtakes him nor sleep. His is all that is in the heavens and all that is on earth'.

Many Muslims visit the mosque to pray. They learn to read and **recite** the **Qur'an**, find out more about their faith and meet their friends. They sit or kneel on the floor on small carpets called prayer mats.

22

Muslims must face towards the holy city of Makkah in Saudi Arabia when they pray. A mosque has a small arch, called a mihrab, in one wall. This mihrab shows the direction of Makkah.

# Door of the Guru

Sikhs meet to worship in a building called a gurdwara. This means 'the door of the Guru'. It is the place where the Guru Granth Sahib, the Sikh holy book, is kept.

Inside the gurdwara, the Guru Granth Sahib rests on a platform under a canopy. This shows how important it is. When worshippers enter the gurdwara, they take off their shoes and cover their heads. They **bow** to the Guru Granth Sahib to show their respect.

Many special family events happen in the gurdwara. Sikh weddings, like this one, take place in the worship room, in front of the Guru Granth Sahib. After the ceremony, everyone shares a meal cooked in the gurdwara kitchen.

The Golden Temple in Amritsar, India, is a very special gurdwara. It was built by Guru Arjan on an island in the middle of a lake. Its golden walls are covered with verses from the Guru Granth Sahib.

# Notes for teachers

**Pages 4 & 5** Hindus believe that the mandir is God's home on Earth. In the holiest part of the mandir, called the inner sanctum, God is represented by murtis, sacred images of the gods and goddesses. Each mandir is usually dedicated to a particular god, goddess or holy person. The murtis are installed according to ancient rituals and treated as living beings. Hindus visit the mandir for a darshana, or 'viewing' of the deity. They take offerings for the deity, which are given through a priest, in return for the deity's blessing. There is no obligation on Hindus to visit the mandir. Some go regularly; others go on festivals or for family celebrations. A mandir is more than simply a place for worship. It plays an important part in the Hindu community, as a meeting place and as a place where children and adults can learn more about their religion.

**Pages 6 & 7** In Britain and other countries where Hindus have settled, mandirs are often housed in converted churches, halls or other buildings. A few are specially built. Traditional temples are constructed according to strict, ancient rules of design and measurement. The murti is installed in the garbhagrha, or 'womb chamber' which symbolizes a dark cave. Above it rises a dome or tower that represents the journey upwards to the sky, from which a person receives divine inspiration. Mandirs range in size from small, portable street temples to huge temple towns.

Every year, millions of Hindu pilgrims flock to the city of Varanasi to bathe and scatter the ashes of dead relations in the sacred River Ganges. This is the most auspicious of seven tirthas, or 'fords'. These are places where Hindus believe you can cross over from this world to moksha, or liberation from the continuous cycle of birth, death and rebirth.

**Pages 8 & 9** The word synagogue means 'meeting house'. It is the main focus of the Jewish community where people meet for worship. Many synagogues also have community halls and synagogue schools attached. The most important part of a synagogue is the Holy Ark, at the front of the synagogue, where the Torah scrolls (the Sefer Torah) are kept. A lamp, called the Ner Tamid, burns constantly outside the Ark as a reminder to Jewish people that God is always present. During worship, the scrolls are taken out of the Ark and placed on a raised platform called the bimah.

In an Orthodox synagogue, men and women sit apart, and men lead the worship. In Progressive synagogues, everyone sits together, and worship is led by men and women.

**Pages 10 & 11** For Jewish people, worship at home is very important, but many Jews also go to the synagogue on Friday evening, the start of Shabbat, or on Saturday. There are special synagogue services at festival times, and for important rites of passage, such as a boy's Bar Mitzvah, a girl's Bat Mitzvah, marriages and funerals.

The Western Wall in Jerusalem is the holiest place for Jews and an important place of pilgrimage. The Wall is all that remained of the Temple after its destruction by the Romans in 70 CE. Jews gather and pray in front of the Wall, where they feel close to God. Prayers are often written on pieces of paper and inserted into cracks in the Wall.

**Pages 12 & 13** A vihara is a place where Buddhists worship and Buddhist monks or nuns live. It is sometimes called a temple or a monastery. Originally, in the early days of Buddhism in India, viharas were simple dwellings where monks sheltered during the rainy season. They later became permanent establishments.

Inside the vihara is a shrine room, dedicated to the Buddha. Here worshippers bow or kneel in front of an image of the Buddha, and leave offerings, to show their respect. The image reminds them of the Buddha's teaching and that, by following his example, they too can reach enlightenment. Buddhists are not obliged to visit the vihara but many do, especially on holy days and festivals.

**Pages 14 & 15** Stupas are dome-shaped shrines, found all over the Buddhist world. In countries such as Japan and China, they have evolved into a distinctive pagoda shape. The earliest stupas were built in India after the Buddha's death, to house his ashes and other personal possessions. Stupas have also been built to hold the ashes of important monks or copies of the sacred texts. These places have also become important sacred symbols. When Buddhists visit a stupa, they walk around it three times in a clockwise direction. This reminds them of the Three Jewels of Buddhism – the Buddha, the sangha (Buddhist community) and the dhamma (the Buddha's teaching).

Zen is a type of Buddhism followed in Japan. The word 'Zen' means 'meditation' and the aim of Zen Buddhists is to achieve enlightenment through meditation. They use gardens, poetry, painting and martial arts to help them.

**Pages 16 & 17** The word church means a place where Christians worship. The word Church, with a capital 'C' means a group of Christians, such as the Roman Catholic Church.

Many churches are built in the shape of the cross, the most important Christian symbol. Inside, some are highly ornate, for example, Orthodox churches are usually richly decorated with icons and paintings. Others are very plain and simple. The altar is the most important part of most churches. This is where the bread and wine are laid out for Holy Communion. Traditionally there is also a reading desk, called a lectern, and a pulpit. Many churches have beautiful stained glass windows which depict stories from the Bible, or holy people, such as saints. A cathedral is the main church in a diocese, the district in which a bishop has his official seat.

**Pages 18 & 19** Christian places of pilgrimage include the Holy Land (Israel and Palestine), where Jesus lived and died, the Vatican City in Rome, and the shrines of important saints, such as that of St James in Santiago de Compostela in Spain. One of the most important places of pilgrimage in Britain is Canterbury Cathedral where St Thomas à Becket was killed in 1170 CE.

The Vatican City is an independent state within the city of Rome. It is the headquarters of the Roman Catholic Church and the home of the Pope. Millions of pilgrims flock to Rome each year, hoping to be seen and blessed by the Pope. The Vatican buildings house many priceless works of Christian art.

**Pages 20 & 21** Muslims can offer prayers to Allah anywhere but many prefer to worship in a mosque. In Arabic, a mosque is called a masjid. Muslims are called to prayer from the minaret by the muezzin, the Muslim crier or by a recording. Many mosques today are equipped with loudspeakers. Muslims always wash before they pray so all mosques have a place for washing. In larger, older mosques this may be a fountain or a pool in the courtyard outside the mosque. Modern mosques usually have washrooms with rows of taps. No pictures or statues of human figures are allowed inside, to prevent people worshipping them instead of Allah. But many mosques are beautifully decorated with inscriptions of verses from the Qur'an and with geometric shapes and patterns. In Islam, calligraphy has become a major art form, with many different styles.

**Pages 22 & 23** Muslims must pray five times a day, at fixed times taught by Muhammad (ﷺ). They do not have to attend the mosque to pray, though many Muslims do visit every day. Muslim men are expected to go the mosque for lunchtime prayers on Friday, the communal day of prayers. The mosque also functions as a social and welfare centre, and as a school where children are taught Arabic and to read the Qur'an. When they pray, Muslims face the holy city of Makkah, the site of the Ka'ba, the most sacred Islamic shrine and the place where Muhammad (ﷺ) first taught people about Allah. The three most important mosques are in Makkah, al-Madinah (also in Saudi Arabia) and in Jerusalem.

**Pages 24 & 25** The word gurdwara means 'the door of the Guru', a way of showing that this building is God's house. It does not have to be a specially designed building. The important thing is that it contains a copy of the Guru Granth Sahib, the 'living' Guru, or teacher, of the Sikhs. When worshippers enter the gurdwara, they remove their shoes, cover their heads and kneel or bow before the sacred book to show their respect. Traditionally, gurdwaras have entrances on all four sides, symbolizing that everyone is welcome. A gurdwara extends a welcome to men and women whatever their religion or origins. This reflects the key Sikh belief – that everyone is equal in God's eyes.

**Pages 26 & 27** The gurdwara is primarily a place where Sikhs gather for worship in the presence of the Guru Granth Sahib. But it also has a vital social function and provides a focus for life in the Sikh community. Festivals, called Gurpurbs, often take place in the gurdwara. Apart from the prayer hall, gurdwaras also have a kitchen, where langar, the communal meal, is prepared. This is eaten in the communal dining room. A yellow and blue flag, called the Nishan Sahib, or respected flag, flies outside the gurdwara. It indicates that the building is a gurdwara. In Britain and other countries where Sikhs have settled, gurdwaras are often established in converted schools, churches and halls.

# Glossary

**altar** A special table used in a Christian church. This is where the bread and wine are placed for the Communion service.

**basilica** A large church building.

**beliefs** Having a belief in something means thinking or trusting that it is true.

**bow** Bending your head or body forwards.

**canopy** A covering, like a roof.

**congregation** A group of people at a service. They congregate, or meet, for worship.

**faith** Another word for a religion, or a set of beliefs.

**holy** Special or precious, or closest to God.

**meditation** Thinking very hard or deeply about something, or clearing your mind so that you feel calm and peaceful.

**monks** Men that live as part of a religious group and have made certain vows (promises).

**nuns** Women that live as part of a religious group and have made certain vows (promises).

**Qu'ran** The Muslim holy book.

**recite** Read out loud, often by heart.

**respects** Paying your respects shows how much you honour or look up to someone.

**scrolls** Rolled-up pieces of paper.

**sins** Bad deeds, or wrong-doings.

**stupas** Domed buildings which are religious shrines.

**worship** To show your love and devotion to God or to the gods.

# Books to read

HINDU
**Diwali** by Kerena Marchant (Wayland, 1996)
**Hindu** by Jenny Wood (Franklin Watts, 1996)
**Hindu Mandir** by Anita Ganeri (A & C Black, 1997)

JEWISH
**The Seventh Day is Shabbat** by Margaret Barratt (Heinemann, 1994)

BUDDHIST
**The Buddha's Birthday** by Margaret Barratt (Heinemann, 1994)
**My Buddhist Life** by Meg St. Pierre and Marty Casey (Wayland, 1996)
**A Buddhist Vihara** by Anita Ganeri (A & C Black, 1997)

CHRISTIAN
**A Christian Church** by Alison Seaman and Alan Brown (A & C Black, 1997)

**Prayers for Children** by Christopher Herbert (The National Society, 1993)
**Lucy's Sunday** by Margaret Barratt (Heinemann, 1994)
**Water into Wine** by Alain Royer and Georges Carpentier (Heinemann, 1998)

SIKH
**I am a Sikh** by Manju Aggarwal (Franklin Watts, 1984)
**My Sikh Life** by Kanwaljit Kaur-Singh (Wayland, 1997)

**General series on religion:**
**Beliefs and Cultures** series (Franklin Watts, 1997/8)
**Everyday Religion** series (Wayland, 1996/7)
**Festivals** series (Wayland 1996/7)
**Introducing Religions** series (Heinemann, 1997)
**Looking at Christianity** series and **Looking at Judaism** series (Wayland, 1998)

Editor: Sarah Doughty
Design: Sterling Associates
Consultant: Alison Seaman

First published in Great Britain in 1998
by Wayland (Publishers) Ltd
Reprinted in 2000 by Hodder Wayland,
an imprint of Hodder Children's Books

© Hodder Wayland 1998
Hodder Children's Books, a division of Hodder Headline Ltd,
338 Euston Road, London NW1 3BH

British Library Cataloguing in Publication Data
Ganeri, Anita
    Religious Buildings. – (What's Special to me?)
    1. Sacred space – Juvenile literature
    I. Title
    291.3'5

ISBN 0 7502 3225 0

Printed and bound by G.Canale & C.S.p.A., Turin

Picture acknowledgements: Axiom Photographic Agency 19 (James Morris); Ann & Bury Peerless 13, 14; Circa Picture Library 10 (Barry Searle), 25 (John Smith); Christine Osborne Pictures 23; Eye Ubiquitous 5 (David Cumming), 6 (John Dakers), 27 (main); Impact 11 (Mark Cator), 12 (both) (Mohamed Ansar), 18 (Penny Tweedie); J. Allan Cash Ltd 16; Peter Sanders 26; Robert Harding Picture Library 15 (Michael Jenner), 21 (Adam Woolfitt); Tony Stone Worldwide 7 (David Sutherland), 22 (Paul Chesley); Topham Picturepoint 9; Trip 27 (inset) (H Rogers); Wayland Picture Library, title page, 3 (Rupert Horrox), 4, 8 (Rupert Horrox), 17 (Chris Fairclough), 20, 24 (Zak Waters)

# Index

Entries in **bold** are pictures